THIS BOOK BELONGS TO:

_____

Dedicated to my Aunt Becky.

All rights reserved.
No part of this book may be reproduced in any form or by any means, electronic or mechanical, and no photocopying or recording, unless you have written permission from the author.

ISBN 978-1-958985-52-6

Text copyright © 2025 by Mimi Jones

www.joeysavestheday.com

A Mimi Book

WELCOME TO THE WONDERFUL WORLD OF EASTER!

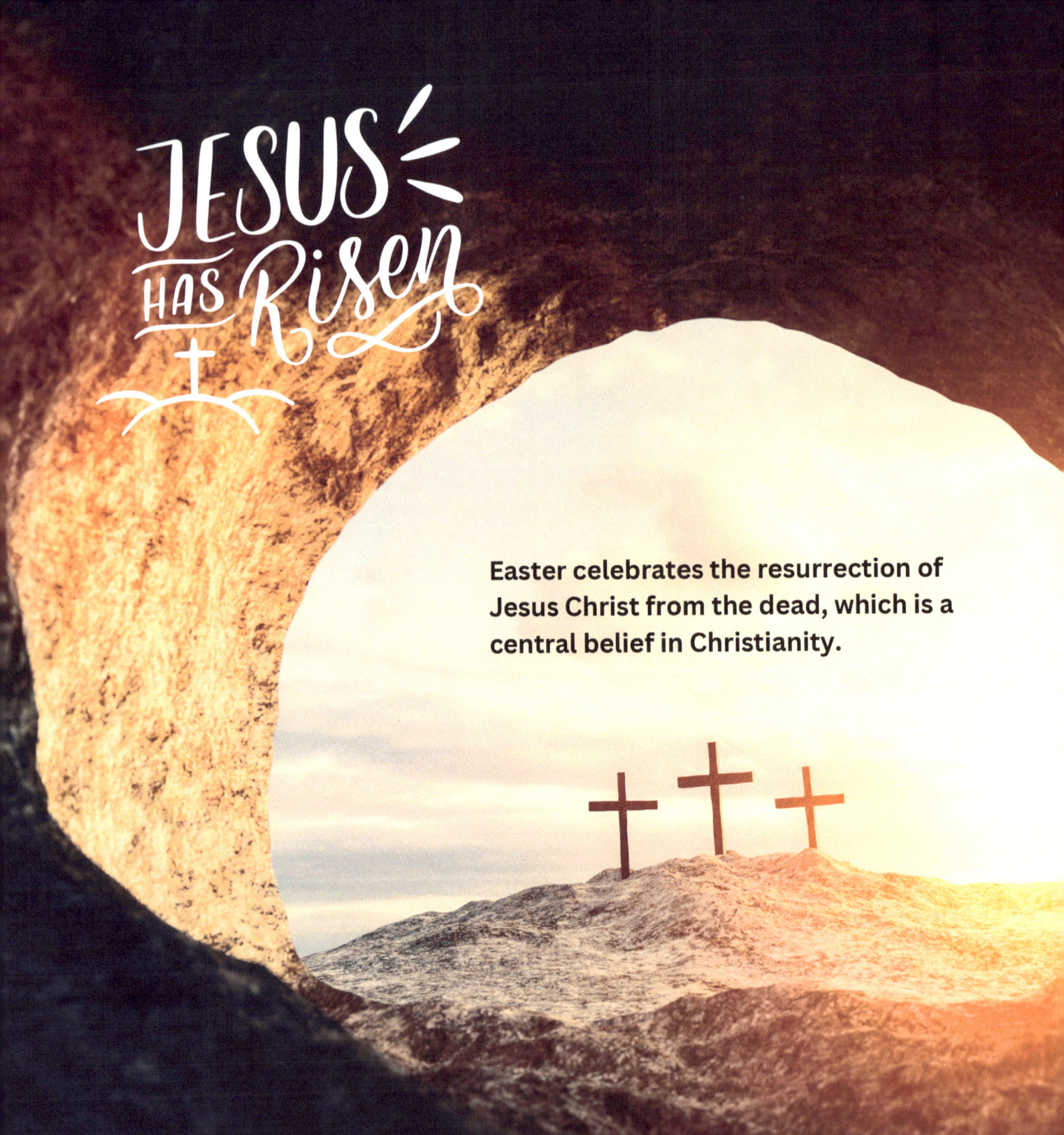

The date of Easter changes every year because it is based on the lunar calendar. It falls on the first Sunday after the first full moon following the vernal equinox.

The week leading up to Easter is called Holy Week, which includes Palm Sunday, Maundy Thursday, Good Friday, and Holy Saturday.

Many churches hold special sunrise services on Easter Sunday to celebrate the resurrection of Jesus.

EASTER SUNDAY

Easter eggs symbolize new life and rebirth.

The Easter Bunny is a popular figure associated with Easter and is said to deliver Easter eggs to children.

The Easter Bunny tradition originated in Germany and was brought to America by German immigrants in the 1700s.

Germany

America

In some cultures, children participate in Easter egg hunts, searching for hidden eggs filled with candy or small toys.

EASTER EGG HUNT!

Another popular Easter activity is egg rolling, where decorated eggs are rolled down a hill or slope.

The White House in Washington, D.C., hosts an annual Easter Egg Roll event on the White House lawn.

EASTER

Many people enjoy eating chocolate eggs and other sweets during Easter. The largest chocolate egg ever made weighed over 15,000 pounds!

Hot cross buns are a traditional Easter treat, marked with a cross on top to symbolize the crucifixion of Jesus.

In Greece, people celebrate Easter with a feast that includes roasted lamb, which represents the Lamb of God.

Greece

In Italy, Easter is celebrated with a special cake called "Colomba," shaped like a dove to symbolize peace.

Italy

In Sweden, children dress up as "Easter witches" and go door-to-door, asking for treats similar to Halloween.

In Australia, the Easter Bilby is a popular alternative to the Easter Bunny, raising awareness for the endangered bilby species.

In Mexico, Semana Santa (Holy Week) is celebrated with elaborate processions, reenactments of the Passion of Christ, and traditional foods.

Mexico

In Spain, people participate in processions featuring religious statues and penitents wearing traditional robes and hoods.

Spain

In the Philippines, some devotees reenact the crucifixion of Jesus by volunteering to be nailed to crosses.

Good Friday

In Bermuda, people celebrate Good Friday by flying kites, symbolizing the ascension of Jesus into heaven.

In the United Kingdom, Morris dancers perform traditional folk dances to celebrate the arrival of spring.

United Kingdom

Count the Easter Eggs.

Thanks a bunch for spending your precious time on this! I hope it tickled your brain and sprinkled some useful nuggets of wisdom into your day!

THE END!

www.ingramcontent.com/pod-product-compliance
Lightning Source LLC
Chambersburg PA
CBHW040029050426
42453CB00002B/60